INSPIRATION

FOR

WRITERS

INSPIRATION FOR WRITERS

Summersdale Publishers Ltd
46 West Street
Chichester
West Sussex
PO19 1RP
UK

www.summersdale.com

Printed and bound in the Czech Republic

ISBN: 978-1-84953-214-3

Substantial discounts on bulk quantities of Summersdale books are available to corporations, professional associations and other organisations. For details telephone Summersdale Publishers on (+44-1243-771107), fax (+44-1243-786300) or email (nicky@summersdale.com).

INSPIRATION

FOR

WRITERS

EMILY DARCY

You don't write because you
want to say something, you
write because you've got
something to say.

F. SCOTT FITZGERALD

Write only if you cannot
live without writing. Write
only what you alone
can write.

ELIE WIESEL

… everything in life is
writable about if you have
the outgoing guts to do it,
and the imagination
to improvise.

SYLVIA PLATH

I begin with writing the
first sentence – and trusting
to Almighty God for
the second.

LAURENCE STERNE

Put it before them briefly
so they will read it, clearly
so they will appreciate it,
picturesquely so they will
remember it, and above all,
accurately so they will be
guided by its light.

JOSEPH PULITZER

The more important virtue
for a writer, I believe, is
self-forgiveness.

ELIZABETH GILBERT

One must be drenched in words, literally soaked with them, to have the right ones form themselves into the proper pattern at the right moment.

HART CRANE

Writing is the geometry
of the soul.

PLATO

Writing is really rewriting
– making the story better,
clearer, truer.

ROBERT LIPSYTE

When I want to read a
novel, I write one.

BENJAMIN DISRAELI

If you want to write, you can. Fear stops most people from writing, not lack of talent, whatever that is.

RICHARD RHODES

Writing is not a job
description. A great deal
of it is luck.

MARGARET ATWOOD

The less conscious one is of being 'a writer', the better the writing.

PICO IYER

… look in thy heart
and write.

PHILIP SIDNEY

Write for the most intelligent, wittiest, wisest audience in the universe: write to please yourself.

HARLAN ELLISON

Immature poets imitate;
mature poets steal.

T. S. ELIOT,
THE SACRED WOOD

I try to leave out the parts
that people skip.

ELMORE LEONARD

It is a delicious thing to write, to be no longer yourself but to move in an entire universe of your own creating.

GUSTAVE FLAUBERT

By writing much,
one learns to write well.

ROBERT SOUTHEY

If you can't annoy
somebody, there's little
point in writing.

KINGSLEY AMIS

The pen is mightier than
the sword, and considerably
easier to write with.

MARTY FELDMAN

… fill your paper with the
breathings of your heart.

WILLIAM WORDSWORTH

Every writer is a thief,
though some of us are
more clever than others at
disguising our robberies.

JOSEPH EPSTEIN

The best time for
planning a book is while
you're doing the dishes.

AGATHA CHRISTIE

It is an excellent discipline for an author to feel that he must say all he has to say in the fewest possible words, or his reader is sure to skip them; and in the plainest possible words or his reader will certainly misunderstand them.

JOHN RUSKIN

The wastebasket is a
writer's best friend.

ISAAC BASHEVIS SINGER

Easy reading is damn
hard writing.

NATHANIEL HAWTHORNE

Yes, the story I am writing exists, written in absolutely perfect fashion, some place, in the air. All I must do is find it, and copy it.

JULES RENARD

If my doctor told me I had only six minutes to live, I wouldn't brood. I'd type a little faster.

ISAAC ASIMOV

A man would do very well
to carry a pencil in his
pocket and write down the
thoughts of the moment.
Those that come unsought
for are commonly the
most valuable…

FRANCIS BACON

Writing comes more easily if
you have something to say.

SHOLEM ASCH

All my best thoughts were
stolen by the ancients.

RALPH WALDO EMERSON

There are no laws for the novel. There never have been, nor can there ever be.

DORIS LESSING

There are three rules
for writing the novel.
Unfortunately, no one
knows what they are.

W. SOMERSET MAUGHAM

Why do writers write?
Because it isn't there.

THOMAS BERGER

I was working on the proof
of one of my poems all the
morning, and took out a
comma. In the afternoon I
put it back again.

OSCAR WILDE

The chief glory of
every people arises from
its authors.

SAMUEL JOHNSON

Writing is 1 per cent
inspiration, and 99 per cent
elimination.

LOUISE BROOKS

A writer is a person for
whom writing is more
difficult than it is for
other people.

THOMAS MANN

I admire anybody who
has the guts to write
anything at all.

E. B. WHITE

… however great a man's natural talents may be, the art of writing cannot be learnt all at once.

JEAN-JACQUES ROUSSEAU

Books want to be born: I never make them. They come to me and insist on being written, and on being such and such.

SAMUEL BUTLER

What no wife of a writer
can ever understand is that a
writer is working when he's
staring out of the window.

BURTON RASCOE

Just leave your mind alone;
your intuition knows what
it wants to write, so get
out of the way.

RAY BRADBURY

Writing a book is
an adventure.

WINSTON CHURCHILL

The purpose of a writer is
to keep civilisation from
destroying itself.

BERNARD MALAMUD

In a writer there must always be two people – the writer and the critic.

LEO TOLSTOY

Forget all the rules. Forget
about being published.
Write for yourself and
celebrate writing.

MELINDA HAYNES

Writing is the incurable itch
that possesses many.

JUVENAL

My aim is to put down on
paper what I see and what
I feel in the best and
simplest way.

ERNEST HEMINGWAY

True ease in writing comes
from art, not chance,
As those who move easiest
who have learned to dance.

ALEXANDER POPE,
'AN ESSAY ON CRITICISM'

If a story is in you, it has
got to come out.

WILLIAM FAULKNER

Every word born of an inner
necessity — writing must
never be anything else.

ETTY HILLESUM

Becoming the reader is
the essence of becoming
a writer.

JOHN O'HAYRE

As to the adjective, when in doubt, strike it out.

MARK TWAIN, *THE TRAGEDY OF PUDD'NHEAD WILSON*

... it is with words as with sunbeams – the more they are condensed, the deeper they burn.

ROBERT SOUTHEY

An original writer is not
one who imitates nobody,
but one whom nobody
can imitate.

FRANÇOIS-RENÉ DE
CHATEAUBRIAND

If there is a book you really want to read but it hasn't been written yet, then you must write it.

TONI MORRISON

To produce a mighty
book, you must choose a
mighty theme.

HERMAN MELVILLE

One ought only to write
when one leaves a piece
of one's own flesh in the
inkpot, each time one
dips one's pen.

LEO TOLSTOY

The faster you blurt, the
more swiftly you write, the
more honest you are.

RAY BRADBURY

An author in his book must
be like God in the universe,
present everywhere and
visible nowhere.

GUSTAVE FLAUBERT

You can only learn to
be a better writer by
actually writing.

DORIS LESSING

The way you define yourself
as a writer is that you write
every time you have a free
minute. If you didn't behave
that way you would never
do anything.

JOHN IRVING

The secret of getting ahead
is getting started.

MARK TWAIN

The six golden rules of
writing: read, read, read,
and write, write, write.

ERNEST J. GAINES

Writing is easy. All you do is stare at a blank sheet of paper until drops of blood form on your forehead.

GENE FOWLER

Writing is the best way
to talk without being
interrupted.

JULES RENARD

If you don't think there
is magic in writing, you
probably won't write
anything magical.

TERRY BROOKS

Prose = words in their best order; poetry = the best words in their best order.

Samuel Taylor Coleridge

Whether or not you write
well, write bravely.

BILL STOUT

The role of the writer is
not to say what we all can
say, but what we are
unable to say.

ANAÏS NIN

I am not at all in a
humour for writing; I must
write on till I am.

JANE AUSTEN

The greatest part of a
writer's time is spent in
reading in order to write:
a man will turn over half a
library to make one book.

SAMUEL JOHNSON

We are all apprentices in a craft where no one ever becomes a master.

Ernest Hemingway

Better to write for yourself
and have no public, than to
write for the public and
have no self.

CYRIL CONNOLLY

I'd rather be caught holding up a bank than stealing so much as a two-word phrase from another writer.

JACK SMITH

If a nation loses its
storytellers, it loses
its childhood.

PETER HANDKE

No author dislikes to be
edited as much as he dislikes
not to be published.

RUSSELL LYNES

Of all those arts in which
the wise excel, nature's chief
masterpiece is writing well.

JOHN SHEFFIELD,
1ST DUKE OF BUCKINGHAM
AND NORMANBY

You can't wait for
inspiration. You have to go
after it with a club.

JACK LONDON

A good style should show
no signs of effort. What is
written should seem a
happy accident.

W. SOMERSET MAUGHAM,
SUMMING UP

Anyone can *become* a writer… the trick, the secret, is to *stay* a writer…

HARLAN ELLISON

You must often make
erasures if you mean to write
what is worthy of being read
a second time; and don't
labour for the admiration of
the crowd, but be content
with a few choice readers.

HORACE

I'm most happy
to be a writer.

MAYA ANGELOU

… of good writing (which, essentially, is clear thinking made visible) precision is the point of capital concern.

Ambrose Bierce

Sit down to write what you
have thought, and not to
think what you shall write.

WILLIAM COBBETT

Be yourself. Above all, let who you are, what you are, what you believe, shine through every sentence you write, every piece you finish.

JOHN JAKES

… write only of what is
important and eternal.

ANTON CHEKHOV,
THE SEAGULL

It is good to have an end to
journey towards; but it is
the journey that matters
in the end.

URSULA K. LE GUIN

INSPIRATION FOR ARTISTS

ISBN: 978-1-84953-215-0

Hardback

£4.99

> *'Every child is an artist. The problem is how to remain an artist once we grow up.'*
>
> **Pablo Picasso**

It is said that a picture paints a thousand words, but sometimes even the most creative people need help to get their artistic juices flowing. This little book, filled with the wit and wisdom of some of the world's most renowned painters, sculptors and other visual artists, is sure to provide inspiration for all who make the world a more beautiful place through their art.

INSPIRATION FOR MUSICIANS

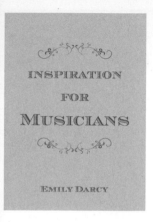

ISBN: 978-1-84953-216-7

Hardback

£4.99

*'Let me write the songs of a nation and
I care not who writes the laws.'*

Plato

Music may be the food of love, but when our melodies
slow down or our harmonies don't fit, we need help to
get back in the flow again. This little book, filled with the
wit and wisdom of some of the world's most renowned
composers and musicians, is sure to provide inspiration
for all who live their life through music.

If you're interested in finding out
more about our gift books, follow us
on Twitter: **@Summersdale**

www.summersdale.com